GUIDES

CATERING

KU-417-972

REAL LIFE GUIDES

Practical guides for practical people

About this series

In this increasingly sophisticated world the need for manually skilled people to build our homes, cut our hair, fix our boilers, and make our cars go is greater than ever. As things progress, so the level of training and competence required of our skilled manual workers increases.

In this new series of career guides from Trotman, we look in detail at what it takes to train for, get into, and be successful at a wide spectrum of practical careers. *Real Life Guides* aim to inform and inspire young people and adults alike by providing comprehensive yet hard-hitting and often blunt information about what it takes to succeed in these careers.

The other titles in the series are:

Real Life Guide to Carpentry and Cabinet-Making

Real Life Guide to Construction

Real Life Guide to Hairdressing

Real Life Guide to Plumbing

Real Life Guide to the Motor Industry

**MORAY COUNCIL
LIBRARIES &
INFO.SERVICES**

20 10 71 23	
Askews	
647.950	

trotman

Real Life

GUIDES

CATERING

Dee Pilgrim

Real Life Guide to Catering
This first edition published in 2003 by Trotman and Company Ltd
2 The Green, Richmond, Surrey TW9 1PL

Editorial and Publishing Team
Author Dee Pilgrim
Series Editor Timuchin Dindjer
Editorial Mina Patria, Editorial Director; Rachel Lockhart,
Commissioning Editor; Anya Wilson, Editor; Erin Milliken, Editorial
Assistant
Production Ken Ruskin, Head of Pre-press and Production
Sales and Marketing Deborah Jones, Head of Sales and
Marketing
Managing Director Toby Trotman

Designed by XAB

British Library Cataloguing in Publications Data
A catalogue record for this book is available from the British
Library

ISBN 0 85660 908 0

All rights reserved. No part of this publication may be
reproduced, stored in a retrieval system or transmitted in any
form or by any means, electronic and mechanical,
photocopying, recording or otherwise without prior permission
of Trotman and Company Ltd.

Typeset by Photoprint, Torquay
Printed and bound in Great Britain by The Cromwell Press,
Trowbridge, Wiltshire.

Real
Life

GUIDES

CONTENTS

About the author

Dee Pilgrim completed the pre-entry, periodical journalism course at the London College of Printing before working on a variety of music and women's titles. As a freelancer and full-time member of staff she has written numerous articles and interviews for *Company*, *Cosmopolitan*, *New Woman*, *Woman's Journal* and *Weight Watcher's* magazines. As a freelancer for Independent Magazines she concentrated on celebrity interviews and film, theatre and restaurant reviews for such titles as *Ms London*, *Girl About Town*, *LAM* and *Nine To Five* magazines, and in her capacity as a critic she has appeared on both radio and television. She is currently the Film Reviewer for *Now* Magazine. When not attending film screenings she is active within the Critics' Circle, co-writes songs and is currently engaged in writing the narrative to an as yet unpublished trilogy of children's illustrated books.

Acknowledgements

Thank you to Ken Hom, Jon Cox, Bill Vickers, Tamas Khan and Jacquie Moon for their contributions to this book.

Special thanks to Springboard for providing information on the hospitality industry, and to Birmingham College of Food, Tourism and Creative Studies for details of its prospectus.

Thanks also to Maria Lockwood at the HCIMA.

Introduction

Eating is one of the great pleasures in life – it's also a necessity. We all have to eat to survive, and yet how many of us, as we sit down in a restaurant to tuck into a delicious piping-hot pizza, or a fabulous five-course feast, ever think just how much effort and how many people it has taken to get that food to our mouths? The catering business is huge – walk down any busy High Street and you will see just how large and varied it really is. You'll probably pass a fast food outlet such as McDonald's or Pizza Express; there may well be one of the pub chains that also serve food, such as the Slug And Lettuce; there might even be a restaurant that boasts Michelin stars. Yet, no matter how varied the quality and price of the food they offer, they have one thing in common: they all need staff.

If you are considering a career in catering, you are doing so at a very exciting time. Never before has there been so much scope for getting on in the industry – mainly because Britain has never

The industry has become more sophisticated and professional in response to people demanding better levels of service, customer care and wider product ranges as they become more knowledgeable about food and drink.

before seen so many new food outlets opening. There are now more than 106,500 restaurants across Britain. This is due to a number of factors, but mainly to social change. With changes in society come changes in our eating patterns. At one time, eating out was considered a great luxury and only for special occasions such as birthdays and anniversaries. Families tended to eat at home, with mum doing the cooking. But with more women going out to work, longer working hours for everyone, more young people leaving the family residence to set up home alone, and the rise in the fast food market, eating out has become an everyday occurrence.

Bill Vickers is the Marketing and Foodservice Manager for the Compass Group, the world's largest and most successful contract foodservice company with brands that include Burger King, Roux Fine Dining and Reef café-bars, and he is well aware of how fast the market has changed. 'Compass has grown from sales of

Out-of-home activities are growing more dynamically than ever before, so the demands for every type of leisure, entertainment, eating and drinking experience are ever increasing.

£450 million a year and 8,000 employees to more than £10 billion and 380,000 employees in ten years,' he says. 'We have only scratched the surface of what potentially can be done during the next decade and we are continually exploring opportunities in our existing avenues of business, while also creating new ones. Out-of-home activities are growing more dynamically than ever before, so the demands for every type of leisure, entertainment, eating and drinking experience are ever increasing. It's not the conventional venues or experiences either: customers want excitement for all the senses. This means more fun and excitement for the people engaged in delivering the service.'

At one time, many people had a poor opinion of a career in catering – many jobs were quite badly paid and catering positions were seen as 'lowly' – but that has changed. Bill Vickers explains: 'The industry has become more sophisticated and professional in response to people demanding better levels of service, customer care and wider product ranges as they become more knowledgeable about food and drink. This drives quality standards up and forces us to understand more about consumer needs and wants.'

At present 1.48 million people around Britain work in the catering industry. They work in well-known outlets, in small, family-run businesses, and in large, expensive restaurants. They also work in less obvious surroundings. Patients in hospitals need to eat. So too do prisoners, schoolchildren and hotel guests, and someone has to prepare and cook their food. And opportunities in catering do not end at the kitchen doors. There are other areas of the catering industry to consider, such as waiting staff, bar staff, wine waiters (sommeliers), maître d's, and managers. This is why catering offers such an exciting career choice for people who are considering their professional futures. The most ambitious may be aiming to follow in Jamie Oliver's footsteps and end up with their own TV show and book contract; others may simply want to cook quality food for their local community. Whatever your own personal ambitions, if you are interested in working in a challenging and expanding market where you get the chance to meet new people and discover new tastes, methods and business practices, then a job in catering may well be just your cup of tea.

This book aims to help you discover whether you are suited for a career in the catering industry. It will help you pinpoint the mental, physical and social skills and strengths you need to get on. It will show you the great range of jobs available in the market, including some you may not have considered or known about before. It will give you practical advice on what qualifications you need and explain the many different options for training. Finally, it will point you in the direction of the main industry and government boards and bodies responsible for that training. In catering, the world really can be your oyster, or crab, or even lobster. It's up to you to make the choice.

KEN HOM

Success story

THE CELEBRITY CHEF

Not content with being a celebrity chef well known for his 12 cookery books and four TV series, 53-year-old Ken Hom is also a director of Noble House Leisure Ltd, a company that owns a whole host of restaurants focusing on different facets of oriental cuisine. These include the Yellow River Café chain, Imperial City, Pacific Orient, Pacific Rim, Sri Siam, Sri Thai City and Sri Nam, which cover everything from traditional Chinese cuisine to a fusion of modern and traditional Thai.

Born in Tucson, Arizona, Ken started cooking at the age of 11, working in his uncle's restaurant in Chicago as a way of supplementing his family's income. At the age of 20, having moved to California, he started giving cookery lessons and realised teaching was where his heart really lay. For almost eight years he taught at the California Culinary Academy and he has just launched the Ken Hom Academy of Oriental Cooking, an in-house programme for employees of Noble House Leisure Ltd to learn all about oriental food preparation. Training is carried out in the kitchens of the company's restaurants and can lead to an NVQ2 – or National Vocational Qualification – in Food

You have to be committed, you have to keep your nose to the grindstone and your eye on the ball. You have to go into it because you love to eat, you love to cook, because you love the whole process of food.

Preparation and Cooking. The NVQ is provided by Noble House and the Hotel and Catering Training Company (HCTC). Ken Hom has just launched another Yellow River Café in York and his new book, *Foolproof Oriental Cookery*, has just been published.

'I basically trained on the job and I don't think I could have learned any other way because I acquired skills while actually working, and that's been very helpful for me and my teaching. Essentially, even with my writing in my books and with my TV series, what I am doing is teaching and that is what I love to do. Now, with the Academy, I want us to get to the summit of what we can achieve, to stretch the possibilities and improve the quality of the work.

DID YOU KNOW?

Celebrity chef Gordon Ramsay started his professional career as a footballer with Glasgow Rangers.

'You really do have to work hard to get on in this business: you can't go into it just to be a star. This is one of the problems with some people coming into catering, they see all these television chefs and they think it is glamorous, but that's the wrong reason to start. Yes, there are now great rewards for some people, but you still have to be committed, you have to keep your nose to the grindstone and your eye on the ball. You have to go into it because you love to eat, you love to cook, because you love the whole process of food. That's terribly important and one thing I try to do when I teach is to inspire my pupils with this passion I have for this profession. You really have to want to eat. You have to be greedy!

'This is not a profession you should go into if you want to have a really good personal life because you will be working long hours. Yet you have to be open to things, you have to read about what's going on in the industry and you have to see the swirl of what is going on around you. I think some of the best chefs I know are those that can talk about any subject. It is important to be well

This is not a profession you should go into if you want to have a really good personal life because you will be working long hours. Yet you have to be open to things, you have to read about what's going on in the industry and you have to see the swirl of what is going on around you.

rounded because that all contributes to the understanding of what is happening.

'Finally, come into the industry with your eyes open and don't have any illusions. Seriously ask yourself if this is something you really are interested in. If the answer is yes then by all means, we welcome you in. Remember, it is more important to love food and to love cooking than to dream of being a star.'

What's the story?

So you've decided you want to enter the busy and exciting world of catering. But do you really know what that world is all about? It is about the chefs and waiters at the local hotel, the waitresses at the Harvester Inn, and the lady preparing all those delicious soups and sandwiches at the deli in the High Street. But it is also about the people preparing the food served at your school and the manager at the staff canteen of the large company down the road. Then there are the outside caterers who prepare all the meals for the actors and technicians on location for films and television, and at large private functions such as marquee weddings, or sporting events such as Royal Ascot. The catering world is actually made up of five sectors:

- hotels
- restaurants
- pubs
- contract catering
- hospitality services.

Of these, it is the restaurant sector that is the largest employer, yet that does not mean working in a restaurant will necessarily mean being employed by a big company. Three-quarters of catering establishments employ fewer than four people. We will be looking at the different aspects of working in each sector and how you can gain entry to them in more detail later in the book, but here you can see the nature of the jobs available in catering.

IN THE KITCHEN

The kitchen is the heart and soul of any catering establishment. It can be a small, compact unit only big enough for two people to work in, or a huge, state of the art workplace fitted with numerous stoves and hobs, and alive with energy and people. Catering is an industry in which employees usually start at the bottom and then, as they gain more experience, work up through the ranks. Starting at the basic level in a kitchen is the kitchen assistant.

KITCHEN ASSISTANT

The kitchen assistant helps to keep the kitchens clean and hygienic, receives deliveries and keeps the stores in order. He or she may also be involved in food preparation.

CATERING ASSISTANT

This is the name given to people who carry out a kitchen assistant's duties but work in the institutional (hospitals, prisons) or contract catering sections (works canteen, motorway service station) rather than in hotels or restaurants. Their involvement in food preparation will be more detailed and they may well find themselves making salads, desserts and sandwiches.

In traditionally run kitchens in restaurants and hotels you then progress to the following levels.

TRAINEE CHEF

The most junior member of a chef's team, the trainee chef gains invaluable experience in all areas of the kitchen. Trainees will be supervised as they learn the basics of cookery, food quality, safety and hygiene, and once judged to be competent (usually after three years) they move up to the position of:

COMMIS CHEF

At commis level, a chef is still very much in training, being supervised while he or she cooks the less elaborate dishes on the menu. It is usually three years before the commis chef will be judged able to move on to the next level:

CHEF DE PARTIE

The partie system is the traditional way in which areas of responsibility are broken down in a kitchen: each chef is responsible for a different section (partie) of the meal. For instance a chef patissier is responsible for desserts, while a chef poissonier deals with fish dishes. The chef de partie will be expected to master each of the different areas and will help to plan menus before becoming a:

SOUS CHEF

With so much experience, the sous chef is responsible not only for food preparation but also for supervising junior staff and taking a certain degree of managerial control over the kitchen, such as ordering in the supplies. He or she acts as deputy to the:

HEAD CHEF

The head chef is responsible for everything that goes on in the kitchen and must liaise closely with the manager of the hotel or restaurant in which they work. They are in charge of their staff, plan the menus and in most establishments will be in charge of the kitchen finances, buying in the raw produce and negotiating with suppliers. Most head chefs have at least 10 years' experience in the industry, but since trainees start so young, you can still make it to head chef before you are 30 years old.

COOK

A cook will have similar duties and responsibilities to a chef, but the level of cooking tends to be more basic. A cook usually works in a contract kitchen such as in a school, a business canteen or a hospital, rather than a hotel or restaurant.

FRONT OF HOUSE

Front of house is where the waiters/waitresses and managers meet, greet and serve food to the public. Here again, people tend to work up through the ranks – even the managers, who need to have intimate knowledge of all aspects of their operation.

WAITER/WAITRESS

Waiters have a vital role to play in catering: they act as the line of communication between the kitchen and front of house. When they take orders from the public it is essential they are accurate, otherwise things can go badly wrong and tempers can get frayed. A waiter must be efficient, but also sociable and friendly. Duties involve setting tables, taking orders, delivering food from the kitchen, clearing tables and delivering the bill.

SOMMELIERS (WINE WAITERS)

The sommelier is not just a bottle opener and pourer, he or she must be really knowledgeable about the wines served in their particular establishment. They must be able to recommend wines to go with certain foods, serve the wine and, in some cases, also look after the wine cellar and do the ordering.

HEAD WAITER

Like the head chef, the head waiter is responsible for the staff under him or her. A head waiter must ensure everything in the restaurant is running smoothly and must sort out problems if they arise. The head waiter must have a close relationship with the restaurant manager as they will co-ordinate staff and service.

RESTAURANT MANAGER

Although restaurant managers rarely serve the food, they often come up through the ranks and so have an intimate knowledge of the duties of their staff. They are responsible for the training and organisation of the waiting staff. They often oversee bookings and make sure things are running smoothly front of house. They must also liaise with the head chef to make sure customers receive their orders efficiently.

IN-BETWEEN

With the rise of the fast food market, there are also now many jobs that cross the boundaries between the kitchen and front of house. Where restaurants have food counters, for example in canteens, delicatessens and motorway service stations, the staff may be asked not only to prepare the food, but also to keep the counter well stocked and to serve the public.

Not all kitchens or restaurants are run in the same way. Often, the breakdown of a person's duties will depend on the number of staff available. In a small country gastropub, the owner may well be doing the cooking with the help of just one kitchen assistant, and the bar staff may serve food as well as drinks. But what every catering outlet needs is well-trained, disciplined staff who know what they are doing. This is why vocational courses are so well established in the catering world and why so many large companies such as Travel Inn, Harvester and All Bar One offer comprehensive training programmes that lead to properly recognised qualifications. It makes sense for them, as they can recruit through their own ranks, and it makes sense for you because you can progress quickly and not get stuck in an entry-level job. In the Training Day chapter (page 47) we will explore in greater detail what types of training are on offer. But before you get into the details of training you need to know if you have the qualities necessary to make it in this industry. The next chapter will help you judge if you have what it takes.

> ## DID YOU KNOW?
>
> Over a third (38.7 per cent) of all staff working in restaurants are aged between 16 and 19.

JACQUIE MOON

Case study 1

THE TRAINEE

A single parent with two children, Jacquie Moon returned to catering after a stint working in childcare. After answering an advertisement in the London Evening Standard, 30-year-old Jacquie got a job working as a waitress for Carluccio's Ltd. There are ten branches of Carluccio's Caffes and Jacquie worked in many of them, quickly rising to the position of supervisor. From here she went on to Carluccio's internally run Management Training Programme, especially designed for staff members. Highly regarded by the industry (Carluccio's has won several Investors in People awards), the programme includes training in every department, so Jacquie has prepared food in the restaurant, served in the bar and delicatessen, and shadowed management shifts. The amount of time the course takes varies from person to person, depending on their skills and abilities, and once fully trained Jacquie will be able to step into the shoes of anyone working at Carluccio's, from a kitchen porter up to the assistant manager.

'Catering is probably the worst job in the world to do if you have commitments of any description, even down to having a relationship or having children. A lot of the time you are doing shift work and that's

This job suits people who don't want to go into an office and see the same faces every day. If you want variety and are lively then this will suit you.

really demanding so you have to enjoy it otherwise it creates a big hole in your life. Sometimes I have to be up at five in the morning and Carluccio's Caffes are open seven days a week so you have to work weekends as well.

'Physically the job is very demanding, you are on your feet throughout the day and it is not always possible to take regular breaks so you have to be a really motivated, energetic person who is prepared to work very hard. I do like being busy though; I could not be confined to a desk. I think this job suits people who

There is a lot of opportunity out there for people. The more hands-on experience you have to offer then the further you will go. You really have to take the bull by the horns and be interested. If you have been well trained and have the knowledge on board then you can really go out and sell yourself.

don't want to go into an office and see the same faces every day. If you want variety and are lively then this will suit you. You also have to like being confronted with problems because when you have 20 people at the front door waiting to be seated, sorted out and back to work by a certain time you can't panic. You have to be organised and be able to think on your feet.

'I love talking to people and love meeting new people. I'm very sociable but you have to accept that your customers are the public and there's a boundary there that you don't cross. You need to be quite thick-skinned because if problems do occur it can get rather heated. My advice is don't take it personally! Having said that, I do like it when I look around and see customers enjoying themselves and know that I am a part of that and am contributing to that.

'Business is booming and I can't see that tailing off. Carluccio's will be opening another five branches in the next year or two. There is a lot of opportunity out there for people. The more hands-on experience you have to offer then the further you will go. You really have to take the bull by the horns and be interested. If you have been well trained and have the knowledge on board then you can really go out and sell yourself. In fact, the catering industry is now becoming very competitive. With more well-trained people coming through, companies can pick the best of the crop so my advice to those who really want to make it in this industry is don't go in and just be a waitress or say to yourself "I want to be a manager", get as much experience in all areas as you can because if you are thrown into a difficult situation and show you can deal with it then you've got one over all the other candidates.

'At the moment I am learning so much that's enough for me. But I would love to have a place of my own. I think that is the goal for a lot of people who work in the industry and is the reward for all the hard, unglamorous work you have to do. A place of your own means you aren't answerable to anyone but yourself and you make the rules and things have to be done your way. A place of your own must be very rewarding.'

Tools of the trade

Food, glorious food – even the thought of plates piled high with fabulous dishes from around the world is enough to make many people's mouths water and for some it becomes a passion so serious they end up actually employed in the food industry. Talking to people who work in catering it soon becomes obvious just how much they love their jobs, but they are under no illusions about what hard work it can be. In this industry, if you are willing to put the hours in and do the hard graft you can move up the employment ladder very quickly, but you really do need to be hungry for it. Being ambitious is just one quality that will help you get on, but there are other qualities, talents and strengths that will help you to progress. Below we list the most important. Think of them as your own personal tools, giving you that added extra on your way to success.

- Many jobs in catering are physically demanding, so it is no wonder that so many people employed by restaurants and pubs are young (over a third of restaurant staff are under 20). You have to be **physically fit** to cope with the work. Chefs and front of house personnel are constantly on their feet, bustling about, especially during the extra busy breakfast, lunch and dinner periods, so you need to have stamina.
- The nature of the industry also means that catering staff often work shifts, so you will have to be able to deal with the physical demands of **getting up extremely early** and of **working well into the night**. For those working in kitchens the physical demands are increased by the fact they operate in very high temperatures, with ovens and hot plates constantly on the go, so the old saying, 'if you can't stand the

heat get out of the kitchen' is absolutely true. Physically, it also helps to be naturally **dextrous**: chefs are constantly chopping and cutting with extremely sharp knives at breakneck speed, so being clumsy can affect your ability to do the job. The same is also true for waiting staff who have to juggle loaded plates and glasses while navigating their way around tables and customers.

- **Mental agility** and **enthusiasm** are just as important as physical agility. Be eager, ask questions, look interested and take a positive attitude towards criticism. People who have more experience than you can teach you so much. Remember, working in catering is not a solitary occupation: people work in teams both in the kitchen and front of house. If you can think on your feet, really listen to other people's advice and take the initiative when you have to, other people in your team will know they can depend on you.

- Catering is a people-oriented industry, so you need to be **lively** and **sociable** in order to get on. Good **communication skills**, an outgoing personality and an ability to remain even-tempered when under heavy pressure are all qualities both kitchen and front-of-house staff should cultivate. Chefs do not work in isolation; they are surrounded by their sous chefs, porters and waiting staff, and must be able to issue clear, precise orders to them all. They also have to deal with their suppliers and managers and explain their needs clearly and concisely. Receptionists, maître d's and waiting staff have to communicate not only with the kitchen staff but also, more importantly, with customers, who expect a high level of courtesy and service, so being a people person will really help you to get on. No one wants to go out to enjoy a lovely meal only for the occasion to be marred by a surly and sour-faced waiter. You really have to enjoy being in a social environment, even when you are working while everyone else is having a good time. You may be coming to the end of your shift, with tired and aching feet, but you need to keep a smile on your face.

- Sometimes it is not so easy to smile when problems occur, but **problem-solving** is a key skill to have. This is because there are endless opportunities for problems to arise. A supplier may let a chef down at the last moment and an alternative must be found quickly; a mix-up with an order can lead to a dissatisfied customer; when three members of staff fall sick on the same day the manager must rearrange shifts in order for a full team to be on hand. Using your common sense and organisational skills to solve these problems practically and with as little fuss as possible increases your value as an employee.

- Possessing a **good sense of humour** will definitely help when you hit problems. The people who rise the quickest in this industry are those who can carry on smiling while their establishment seems to have been hit by a tornado. Even if World War III erupts behind the kitchen doors, if you can keep your customers happy and satisfied then you've got what it takes to succeed.

- Hygiene is of the utmost importance when you are working with food, especially when you are catering for large numbers of people. Employers will be more inclined to take on staff with **good personal hygiene**. This is not only true of those working in the kitchen, but also of those members of staff who have general contact with the public. Washing regularly and having clean hair and, especially, hands and fingernails (which should be kept trimmed short), indicates that not only do you care about your appearance, you also care about cleanliness.

- The world of catering is a fluid and quickly changing environment where fads and trends can come and go almost overnight. A decade ago Thai food and restaurants were almost unknown in Britain, while ingredients such as lemongrass and lime leaves were unheard of. Now you can even find them on the shelves of your local supermarket. These changes in food fashions make a career in catering very exciting, but also mean you have to keep your eye on the ball in order to keep up with them. So being **open to new ideas**, being aware of what is going on and sustaining your interest are all vital whether you want to be a world class chef or manage your own bar.

While these qualities and skills will help you to get on, there are also weaknesses and physical conditions that could hold you back. There are also downsides to working in the business that may make it unsuitable for you personally. You should take the following into consideration before embarking on a training course in catering, especially those based in the kitchen.

- If you are prone to **fainting fits** or **dizzy spells in extreme heat** you may well find the intensely hot atmosphere in a busy kitchen is just too much for you to take. A trainee with the famous Roux Brothers once described the physical conditions of cooking in their kitchen as being like a miner working on a coal face deep in a badly ventilated mine shaft.
- Those with serious **food allergies** are probably only too well aware of the dangers certain foods can pose. If you are a chef you constantly taste the food you are preparing – which could be life-threatening for those with a nut or fish allergy.
- If your **religious beliefs** ban certain foods you will have to look long and hard at whether a job in catering is for you. For instance, both the Jewish and Muslim faiths forbid eating pork and bacon. Those following a strict vegetarian regime would not be able to handle the meat and fish found in so many dishes. Obviously, there are specialist restaurants that cater for different diets, but you need to ask yourself how severely this would restrict you from progressing in the industry.
- All jobs in catering will involve being on your feet for most of your shift. This can cause health problems for some people and is one reason why so many waitresses wear support tights in order to guard against getting 'heavy legs' and varicose veins in later life. People who have a family or personal history of **back problems** should also be aware that being a chef or waiter involves a lot of bending, stooping,

picking up and putting down that can lead to stiff shoulders
and necks and more serious back conditions.

- People in catering do not work regular nine-to-five hours – not
even the management – so if you are looking for a job where
you are free in the evenings, at weekends and over the big
holiday periods (Christmas, Easter) this is definitely not the
industry for you. Your shift pattern can also change seasonally,
depending on the volume of customers at your establishment.
For example, the Sports Café bar in London's Haymarket was
recently granted Britain's first ever long-term 24-hour licence,
in order to serve people wanting to watch the Rugby World
Cup being beamed live on TV from Australia. The time
difference means games will kick off between 4.30am and
9am London time, and the licence will enable the bar, with
its 140 staff operating three shifts, to serve food and drink to
eager rugby fans. A career in catering means working while
your friends are out socialising and you will have to make
alternative arrangements to see them. Of all the downsides to
the industry, **unsocial hours** is the one most people cite as
the biggest problem.

- Although by law all kitchen and waiting staff should have
regular breaks, the reality is that if the establishment they work
in suddenly gets very busy it will be a question of 'all hands on
deck'. Because of this, many catering staff find it **impossible
to eat regularly**. Sometimes it will be a question of grabbing
something and eating 'on the hoof' to keep going. Much of
the time you will find yourself eating at the beginning or end of
a shift, hours before or after everyone else has eaten. This can
play havoc with blood sugar levels and if you are diabetic it is
something you really have to keep your eye on.

- Finally, don't panic! If your first instinct in a crisis is to run out
of the door and never come back, or sit down, hyperventilate
and burst into tears, then catering is really not for you. The
preparation and serving of food often seems to hit one crisis
after another so you have to learn to cope with the **pressure**.
This is because problems have to be rectified immediately. If

your restaurant is full of customers and your electricity goes off, you have to deal with it. If a catering company is organising a wedding in a marquee and there is a sudden thunderstorm, they can't send everyone to the pub instead. The ability to stay calm, think it through and sort it out proves you have what it takes to make it – and if you can do so and manage to retain your sense of humour, so much the better.

Now you should have a better idea of whether catering is the industry for you. If you are still keen on a job in this area, try this short quiz of general knowledge questions and scenarios that could crop up while working. Simply choose the answer you think is right or closest to what your own response would be. Seeing how you do will show you if your knowledge is as good as you think it is, but don't worry if you get some answers wrong: this is meant to be fun! Answers are at the end of the quiz.

1. Hollandaise, mint, and béarnaise are all types of:

    A. Herb?
    B. Sauce?
    C. Tea?

2. You are working in the kitchen and an order comes in for a steak done medium rare. The waitress comes back saying the customer says it is overcooked. Do you:

    A. Say it is perfectly cooked, turn it over and send it back out?
    B. Think the customer is always right so start again from scratch?
    C. Go into a huff and refuse to cook for the customer again?

3. Tapas is:

    A. A Greek dance?
    B. A type of sherry?
    C. Small dishes of olives, fish and meat served with drinks in Spain?

4.   You are the most senior waitress working on your shift and in an unfortunate accident some olive oil has been spilled on a customer's suit jacket. He is demanding £200 compensation. Do you:

A. Laugh and say he must be joking?
B. Tell him he will have to write to head office to get it sorted out?
C. Personally guarantee to take the jacket to a specialist dry cleaners, have it cleaned, and then send it back to him?

5.   If a pasta dish is 'al dente' it means it is:

A. Covered in a cream sauce.
B. Slightly firm when you bite into it.
C. Shaped like teeth.

DID YOU KNOW?

One in five new jobs is in the hospitality and leisure industry.

6.   It is the end of a lively evening and a large and raucous group is questioning some items on its bill. One man in particular is getting quite argumentative. Do you:

A. Have a stand-up argument with him there and then?
B. Take him to one side, sit him down with a coffee and reason with him slowly and surely?
C. Take the contested items off the bill but ban the group from ever returning to the bar?

7.   Rump, T-bone and fillet are all types of:

A. Mushroom.
B. Pork.
C. Steak.

8.   You are the youngest chef in the kitchen and the head chef has just told you off in no uncertain terms about the quality of your vegetable preparation. Do you:

A. Argue with him, saying he is being unfair?
B. Take on board what he is saying and try to do better?
C. Just give up?

9. Would you ever use a blowtorch in the kitchen?

A. Yes, to do DIY with.
B. No, think of all that gas!
C. Yes, a specialist blowtorch can be used to caramelise sugar on desserts.

10. Balsamic, cider and malt are all:

A. Alcoholic drinks.
B. Types of vinegar.
C. Varieties of apple.

ANSWERS
1. B. Although mint is a herb and can be made into both a sauce and tea, hollandaise and béarnaise are sauces.

2. B. Of course, the customer isn't always right, but in this case you have to serve them a steak to their preferred taste. As you cannot un-cook the steak, the only solution is to cook a new steak for a shorter time.

3. C. Tapas are Spanish snacks served with drinks. The word actually means 'lid' and refers to the fact the snacks were traditionally served on small plates that were placed over the top of your glass like a lid.

4. C. This is an actual scenario. The waitress kept her cool and explained she could not just give the man £200, but would handle the situation personally by taking the jacket to the dry cleaners and ensuring its safe return to its owner. The result was one satisfied customer and a waitress headed for a management position.

5. B. The word dente means tooth in Italian. In Italy the preferred way to serve pasta is so that as you bite into it, it still feels slightly firm to the teeth.

6. B. No one in catering should have to take abuse from the public but inevitably, after a long evening of drinking, some people can become difficult to handle. This is where your people skills must come in. If you have tact and sensitivity, the situation can be defused. The worst thing to do is to lose your temper too. However, sometimes people just cannot be reasoned with and at this stage, as a final solution, you may have to ban or bar people.

7. C. These are three of the better-known cuts of beef. You can get pork fillets, but you can't get pork T-bone!

8. B. No one likes a smart Alec, especially not in a busy kitchen where there is no time for the head chef to argue with you or keep correcting your mistakes. Remember, you are there to learn, so be eager to take any advice or tips you are given. The more enthusiastic you are, the quicker you will get on.

9. C. A specialist chef's blowtorch is just one of the many and varied kitchen tools and utensils now employed in the modern professional kitchen. You will need to learn how to recognise them and to use most of them.

10. B. Although cider is indeed an alcoholic drink as well as being a type of apple, all three are forms of vinegar used for anything from mixing with olive oil as a salad dressing (balsamic), to sprinkling on your chips (malt).

Having completed this section of the book you should have a better idea of whether you have the skills, basic knowledge, and, most importantly, the desire to enter the world of catering. Making Your Mind Up (page 39) looks at what the job can do for you in financial, personal and social terms.

5

A day in the life of an executive chef

Forty-one-year-old Tamas Khan joined the Jim Thompson's chain of Oriental restaurants in 1997 as a wok chef. Since then, he has worked his way up to be Executive Chef for all 14 branches of Jim Thompson's and is responsible for creating a new range of healthy eating dishes recently introduced into the restaurants.

'I start at about ten o'clock every weekday when I go into the office I have above the Jim Thompson's in Putney. Here, I will go through all the mail and emails and do my planning for the week. I phone everybody including my suppliers and then I ring every branch of Jim Thompson's and talk to the managers and the head chefs and find out if they are having any problems.

'I don't get out of the office until about four o'clock in the afternoon and I choose one branch to go and visit. I'll get there at about five and stay until seven, and in that time I will sit down with the chef and have a chat about staff holidays or shortages

Running 14 kitchens is not a one-man job and you need to get everybody behind you so I treat my staff like family and friends. They all have my mobile number and they can call me 24 hours a day.

and we will also have a look at the kitchen to see if it is being kept clean properly and to check the cleaning schedule and log book. Running 14 kitchens is not a one-man job and you need to get everybody behind you so I treat my staff like family and

I pop up to New Covent Garden Market around midnight and spend a few hours talking to my vegetable suppliers, checking the quality and the prices, and seeing what is new.

friends. They all have my mobile number and they can call me 24 hours a day. Sometimes they call me at two in the morning because they need to place an order urgently and they can't get through to the supplier by fax, so I have to ring the supplier direct.

'At around eight in the evening, just before the restaurant I'm visiting that day really starts to kick off, I go and talk to the manager and to the floor staff and watch the food coming down to see if it is up to standard. Once I've checked everything is all right, I may go and visit another branch to see how busy they are and pop in to check how the takeaway service is going. I'd say 65 per cent of my job is spent in the kitchens talking to people.

'Three times a month I meet up with suppliers. If I finish in a restaurant at ten in the evening there is no point me going home to bed, so I pop up to New Covent Garden Market around midnight and spend a few hours talking to my vegetable suppliers, checking the quality and the prices, and seeing what is new. If I visit my meat supplier I like to ask where the meat is from, how it is produced, what does it eat, and how it is slaughtered. I don't get home until the early hours and that is when most of the restaurants close up. I still have to be available as this is when the chefs go through their fridges and see what they need to re-order, so they may need to phone me.

'At the weekends I do something I love. Saturday night I'll walk into any of our branches, put a jacket on and go to work in the kitchen. It gives me more of an idea how my teams are actually working and lets me see if everyone is happy, and it also helps when I set about creating a new menu because I can check to see if new dishes are achievable in each different kitchen.

'I have a few hours off on a Sunday to do things like my laundry, but basically I work a seven-day week, and I love it!'

6

Making your mind up

By now, you will be aware that catering is a service industry in which you, the employee, offer a service to the wider public, whether they are students in a school canteen, tired travellers at a motorway service station, or well-heeled diners in an expensive restaurant. Your care and attention enriches their lives, but how will working in this sector enrich yours? What will a job in catering bring to your life? Below is a list of common questions people joining the industry ask: the answers may help you to decide whether catering is really for you.

ONCE QUALIFIED, CAN I MOVE UP THE PROMOTION LADDER QUITE QUICKLY?

In catering you most certainly can. It is not uncommon to find people in their twenties already in supervisory and management positions. You can reach the position of head chef by your middle twenties and as the industry keeps expanding there are many opportunities for moving on or sideways. You can choose to specialise and diversify into other sectors such as sales and marketing, facilities management and finance and accounting.

WHAT WILL MY TYPICAL HOURS BE?

In this industry, there are no 'typical' hours. The very nature of the business means working flexible hours is the norm. Most chefs do work a basic 40-hour week, but this will usually be topped up with overtime. Many people in the industry do straight shifts or work split shifts (two separate periods of work during the course of a day). If you work in a restaurant or bar you will normally be working late hours as well, and you will probably be working weekends and public holidays. In contract catering, such as preparing school meals or running a works canteen, hours are likely to be more 'normal', and employees may work Monday to Friday. Outside catering, such as for large sporting events or film location work, can be extremely varied, as such events can last for a single day, over a weekend, or for several weeks or months. As with many other service industries, Christmas and the New Year are the busiest times in catering, with special parties being organised, such as the now traditional office party, and more people treating themselves to a meal out, so you will probably be expected to work at this time.

WILL I GET TIME OFF FOR HOLIDAYS?

Yes, you will. Just don't expect it to be over Christmas! Some establishments do, in fact, close for the holiday period, but many others do not because they are so busy. However, after this hectic time, January is usually pretty quiet, which is why so many people in the catering trade take their holidays in January. The average holiday entitlement is around four weeks a year, but this will obviously depend on who you work for and in what capacity.

HOW MUCH CAN I EXPECT TO EARN?

Pay will depend on experience and expertise. Traditionally, trainee chefs and waiting staff were poorly paid for the hours they put into the job. However, as the profile of the industry has improved,

DID YOU KNOW?

Over 60 per cent of the catering workforce in Britain is female.

so too have pay and conditions. As a commis (junior) chef you would be earning about £9,300, rising to between £11,400 and £16,500 for a chef de partie. Head chefs earn around £18,800 to £26,000, although many celebrity chefs (especially those with Michelin stars) earn a great deal more than that. Skilled waiting staff earn between £10,000 and £20,000, depending on seniority, and they can supplement their incomes with tips. These days many establishments pool the tips and share them out between the whole staff. Because of the increased responsibilities of the position, at management level you could be earning anything between £40,000 and £50,000, but you will earn considerably more if you have responsibility for multi-sites or a whole group of premises.

Further information on salaries can be found at www.maydayexec.co.uk (see Clients scetion for 2003 salary review) and www.berkeley-scott.com (see Jobseekers section). Remember other benefits may include uniform, meals on duty, live-in accommodation and staff discounts.

WILL I BE ABLE TO USE MY SKILLS ABROAD?

Yes, you will. In fact huge numbers of British chefs and other catering staff are working all around the world as you read this. If you are employed in the kitchens of one of the large international hotel chains it is quite normal to spend time gaining experience in their hotels abroad. Many of Britain's best chefs have worked in such diverse places as Switzerland, Dubai, Hong Kong, France and America. As a UK citizen you have the right to work in any of the other European Union countries and there is a Young Workers' Exchange Programme for those aged between 18 and 28. This allows you to get some vocational training or work experience in another EU country for a period of time between three weeks and 16 months. Some people travel as part of their work, for example, preparing high-quality food on cruise liners, or for airlines or the railway. However, the places are limited and competition for them is high. If you think working abroad could be a career choice for you, you should consider doing foreign language GCSEs.

> Your care and attention enriches their lives, but how will working in this sector enrich yours?

WHAT CAN I EXPECT TO GET OUT OF THE INDUSTRY PERSONALLY?

The chance to meet a broad range of people, great variety on the job, and a real sense of achievement. With society's interest in food and all things foodie at an all-time high, there has never been a more exciting time to get into the catering industry. Every day there are new things to learn, new people to meet, and new challenges to rise to. The one thing you won't be is bored, because this is a hectic and physically demanding career. Catering is a 'people' business and one of the most rewarding aspects of the job is the way you really do become part of a team. The other people you work with in your restaurant, bar or cafeteria are not only work colleagues, they are also the friends you will rely on when problems arise or you hit a particularly busy patch.

HOW WILL THE WIDER PUBLIC PERCEIVE ME?

As a professional doing them a service they are grateful for. Unfortunately, there will always be the occasional awkward customer, but for most people out to enjoy a lovely meal or a night on the town, the service you provide adds to their pleasure, and 'thank yous' will far outweigh any complaints. At one time there was a social stigma about being 'in service', but this is no longer true. As the industry continues to expand, standards continue to rise, and people from all walks of life find themselves working in catering. It is now seen as a highly professional career.

EVENTUALLY, COULD I BE MY OWN BOSS?

You most certainly could. Many chefs and managers dream of eventually running their own establishment, maybe a sleepy country pub with great food, a small family-run hotel, or a snazzy French restaurant in the centre of town. Owning your business is a huge responsibility, not least as far as money management is concerned (you will be responsible for everything from paying the wage bills to sorting out building costs and maintenance and complying with legislation). Because of this, many people who want to own their own establishment decide to take further qualifications to increase their management and business skills. The Hotel and Catering International Management Association (HCIMA) offers both a Professional Certificate and a Professional Diploma, which are open to people once they have reached management level and which are taken while on the job. You can learn more about HCIMA in the Resources section of this book (page 65).

7

JONATHAN COX

Case study 2

THE MANAGER

During his years in the catering industry, 42-year-old Jonathan Cox has worked in many different locations and capacities. When he was growing up Jon's mother owned a restaurant and since he knew he wanted to go into the same industry he took a degree in Hotel Management at North London Polytechnic. From there he went on to be an operations manager for Trust House Forte, and then ran his own 14-room hotel and restaurant in Wales, called the Beacons, where he also did much of the cooking. Returning to London, he helped open and manage one of the first generation of gastropubs, the Havelock Tavern in west London. This proved a great success, but Jon wanted to be even more hands-on with his own business. He is now a director of Spatchcock Inns and recently opened a gastropub called the Earl Spencer in south west London. With a rolling menu that changes daily and a bustling bar area it has already proved a great hit with locals and Jon has plans to develop the Earl Spencer even further by opening an upstairs function room where he can host fine dining evenings.

'Having an interest in what I do was absolutely fundamental to me for getting into this industry. There's the old cliché of

You need to enjoy being around people and you have to be prepared to work at unsocial times, which is absolutely crucial. Remember, you will be working while everyone else is out playing.

"you've got to love what you do", but it's absolutely true of catering. You have to enjoy being in a social environment where people are coming out to have a good time and that should really shape your view of what you are doing. You need to enjoy being around people and you have to be prepared to work at unsocial times, which is absolutely crucial. Remember, you will be working while everyone else is out playing. It's a lifestyle thing so be prepared to put in the hours.

'You have to enjoy the thrill of creating something new, right now. Food is now – you are not sitting at a desk writing a masterpiece or turning a lathe and producing a car part, you are creating

Catering has not always been highly regarded as a career here in Britain but attitudes are changing, especially when your local community can see what you bring to the area in terms of the jobs you generate and also the fact you have created a really nice place for local people to enjoy.

something against a deadline where the time pressure is really acute. Because of that you need to be practical and aware. You need to have a degree of common sense and to act on your own initiative because dealing with people is different all the time. It's not just one process; it's lots of different situations and interactions.

'As a manager I have to come in every day and talk to my chef and the rest of my staff to make sure they are OK, then look at the venue to make sure nothing is broken, and then deal with the business side such as checking money, answering correspondence, ordering, talking to people on the phone and all the other admin jobs. Finally, I like to be here when our customers are in because I want to be there for the service, that's what I do. I want to be the guy fronting the whole operation.

'Catering has not always been highly regarded as a career here in Britain but attitudes are changing, especially when your local community can see what you bring to the area in terms of the jobs you generate and also the fact you have created a really nice place for local people to enjoy. I hope we will be here at the Earl Spencer for many years and become even more involved with the community because networking is all part of the job.

DID YOU KNOW?

There are 181,926 waiters and waitresses and 216,717 chefs working in the UK.

'Leisure time is on the way up as is people's disposable income and people will always need to go out in hard times as well as in good times so there will always be jobs in this industry. There are loads of opportunities, the larger companies like Hilton International employ lots of people and there is always the chance to travel as well. The skills you need to get on in catering are a good set of skills to have. If you want to come into this industry, then do think about it carefully. There are downsides but then again, if you want to go into something where you can rise through the ranks pretty quickly and have an awful lot of fun and fulfilment out of, then it is a good thing to do.

'One of the best bits of advice I can give to young people is go and get yourself a Saturday job or after-school job in a restaurant to see if it really is for you. At 14 I worked as a washer-upper to give me some pocket money when I was at school. I remember I bought my first motorbike by being a grill chef in a steak house one summer holiday and that was good fun and confirmed I really did like the business. So, go and get yourself some practical experience and see whether you enjoy it or not. Whether it's working in a teashop in a little market town or working in a hotel, it's nice to go and have a crack at something.'

8

Training day

The previous chapters should have given you a pretty good idea of whether a career in catering is for you or not. If you are certain that it is, the next thing you will have to consider is how you enter the industry. Because catering is such a dynamic and quickly expanding sector, there are now many ways in which you can get industry-recognised qualifications. These can make your progression through the ranks much easier and faster, and if you are serious about getting to the top of the profession they will definitely help you achieve your goal.

There are two main routes for getting into the industry and you should think about them both carefully before deciding which is right for you. Because so much of catering entails being hands-on, one of the best routes is to get a job or become a trainee. By doing so you learn your skills at the cutting edge, and you can gain qualifications at the same time. These could be National Vocational Qualifications or Scottish Vocational Qualifications (NVQs/SVQs), Modern Apprenticeships (MA), or a part-time college course such as the HCIMA Advanced Certificate in Hospitality Studies. Training programmes are usually run either by the employer alone, or by an organisation together with the employer, to provide both training on the job, which is supervised by a specialist, and training off the job at a college or training centre (either day or block release, or one or two evenings a week). The length of the programme varies from a few months to two years. Many of the larger emloyers, such as Carluccio's, Aramark, Pizza Express and Jury's Doyle Hotels, now run their own industry-recognised training programmes, giving you the chance to earn as you learn. The employer benefits because new staff are getting trained to their own specifications, making it much easier to recruit and promote from within the organisation.

The benefits to you are that you are actually employed and earning wages, and you are gaining qualifications that will improve your career prospects and job security.

Alternatively, you could take a full-time college course. Most full-time courses last one or two years and consist of a number of modules that cover different aspects of the job. Most of these courses will lead to NVQs/SVQs from the most basic, Level 1, up to Level 4. Some universities and colleges also offer degree courses in Hospitality and Leisure and related subjects. There are a number of private colleges that also offer courses in catering: however, these can be very expensive and if you do decide to attend one you must check that the qualifications they offer are recognised by the industry.

The most popular industry-recognised qualifications are NVQs/SVQs, where you are assessed on a continuous basis and which are awarded at four different levels. How long it takes you to complete each level will depend on how quickly you complete each unit of work, but many colleges offer full-time courses that cover both NVQ 1 and NVQ 2 and which last one year.

- Level 1 is an introduction to the job and ensures you have the basic skills, including hygiene.
- Level 2 is for more skilled workers who already know the basics. With this level you can enter the catering industry in a junior position.
- Level 3 is for workers with greater responsibilities who can cook much more sophisticated dishes and who may well be supervising other staff. You should have NVQ 3 if you want to apply for a chef's job.
- Level 4 is for those who wish to enter management or become a head chef.

There are two main levels to the Modern Apprenticeship scheme.

- Foundation Modern Apprenticeship (FMA), or Skillseekers in Scotland. This is equivalent to NVQ or SVQ Level 2 and because you are working at the same time as learning it usually takes about eighteen months to complete.
- Advanced Modern Apprenticeship (AMA) is equivalent to NVQ Level 3 and normally takes between two and two and a half years to complete.

MAs are really aimed at school leavers and young people between the ages of 16 and 24. You are eligible for funding only if you finish your MA by the age of 25. There is also a Graduate Apprenticeship (GA). This is only available to people who have already graduated in a non-hospitality discipline and, like the other MAs, it combines work-based learning with higher education. A GA usually takes between 12 and 18 months to complete. The maximum cost of this course is £1,125, but it is income-linked, so if you are earning less than £22,000 your local education authority will pay.

There are other courses you can take, including:

- City and Guilds. As the leading provider of vocational qualifications in the United Kingdom, City and Guilds offers all types of catering courses, including Food Preparation and Cooking, Catering and Hospitality, and Professional Cookery. There are five levels of City and Guilds, Level 1 being the most basic and Level 5 the most advanced, and they are roughly equivalent to levels 1–4 of NVQ/SVQ. City and Guilds Levels 2 and 3 are roughly equivalent to the Foundation MA and the Advanced MA.
- BTEC HNC/HND. Edexcel now administers the Higher National Certificate (HNC) and Higher National Diploma (HND) awards. These qualifications tend to be for people who want to go into management or who want to enter catering at a higher level. For example, to take the HND Hospitality

Business Management programme you need to have
completed NVQ Level 3.

● Hotel and Catering International Management Association
(HCIMA). The HCIMA is the only UK and international
professional management association for individuals working
in the hospitality, leisure and tourism industries. It welcomes all
students into membership as Affiliate Members and enables
those with relevant industry qualifications and experience to
progress through its grades of membership. The HCIMA
website (www.hcima.org.uk) has a special Student Zone
dedicated to helping students find the right courses in the
industry.

Further information on who to contact for these courses is
contained in the Resources chapter (page 65).

Although it is not essential to have paper qualifications to enter
the industry, you will need some qualifications to get on to certain
courses. For example, at Birmingham College of Food, Tourism
and Creative Studies, there are no formal entry requirements to
take NVQ Level 1 Preparing and Serving Food. However, if you
take NVQ Level 3 Advanced Food Preparation and Cooking
Certificate in Food Hygiene you will need to have NVQ Level 2
Basic Food Preparation or an equivalent qualification. Whatever
further education route you decide to take, it will be very useful to
have GCSEs or Scottish Highers in English, Maths and a craft
skill such as Home Economics. If you are thinking of working in
the tourist area or abroad, modern languages are also helpful.
Bear in mind that some college courses do require a minimum of
four GCSE passes.

Getting good grades isn't the only thing you can do while still at
school that will improve your chances of getting on in the
industry. By far the best thing you can do – and all the
professionals who have contributed to this book wholeheartedly
agree – is to get some experience actually working in a catering

environment. Arrange a Saturday job or holiday job with a hotel, restaurant, fast food outlet or private catering company. Even if your only duties are washing up and putting away you will get a taste of what really goes on and have the opportunity to watch what the trained members of staff actually do. This will really help you to decide if this is the career for you; and if you decide to take a vocational route, such as an MA into the industry, a prospective employer will be interested to see it included on your Personal Development Plan (PDP).

As anyone who ever turns on the TV these days knows, food and cooking are tremendously in vogue at present. There are numerous magazines and books out there offering both recipes and facts about food. Show your interest by either buying magazines or borrowing cookery books from the library and actually trying out the recipes at home. Keep up with the latest new ingredients and cooking techniques and by watching cookery shows on TV – it's surprising how much you can learn from the likes of Jamie Oliver, Delia Smith and Nigella Lawson. Also read the local papers: they will have news stories on catering premises opening in your area and you will be able to find out if they have any trainee places available by contacting them direct or by talking to your careers teacher or advisor. The Department of Culture, Media and Sport is sponsoring Career Compass, a showcase for the hospitality and leisure industries. Its website (www.careercompass.co.uk) is a good place to discover which companies in the sector offer on-the-job training.

> **DID YOU KNOW?**
>
> By 2006, 400,000 new jobs will be created in the hospitality and leisure sector.

Career Compass is part of the brilliant Springboard website (www.springboarduk.org.uk). Springboard UK specifically promotes careers in hospitality, leisure and travel and it has a network of centres across the country where over 14,000 people a year get free advice. It publishes some great magazines and pamphlets packed with information, and has direct links to the industry as well as schools and colleges. Each year it runs a national cookery competition called Futurechef for 12- to 14-year-olds, as well as a week-long Careers Festival, all of which can help to make you more prepared for a career in the industry.

Across the country, many colleges have become Centres of Vocational Excellence (COVEs) in specific subjects. For example, Westminster Kingsway College is the COVE for the catering industry in London. You should ask your careers teacher or officer if there is a COVE for catering in your area. Alternatively, check out the website (www.dfes.gov.uk/cove). You should also check to see what courses are available. There are so many different options – from Basic Bakery to Advanced Cake Decoration, from Advanced Food Service to Restaurant Management – that you need to know what is available and what you will be able to apply for. Once again, your careers teacher should be able to advise you, or you can check the websites of the bodies that award vocational qualifications (listed in Resources, page 65) to see what courses best suit your needs and abilities.

Opposite is an easy to follow guide summarising all the information contained in this chapter, from entry level right up to the most senior positions.

access to

CATERING

NO QUALIFICATIONS	ENTRY LEVEL QUALIFICATION
	FOUR GCSEs (A-D) grades 1-3 **GNVQ/GSNVQ** level 1 *selection interview*

ON THE JOB TRAINING

APPRENTICESHIP ✦ TRAINEE SCHEMES

ADVANCED MODERN APPRENTICESHIP (England) SKILLSEEKERS (Scotland) MODERN APPRENTICESHIP (NI) MODERN APPRENTICESHIP (Wales)	e.g. HCIMA (Hotel & Catering International Management Association)

e.g.
FOOD SERVICE ASSISTANT
CHEF/COOK
COUNTER ASSISTANT
KITCHEN ASSISTANT

CREDITS/FURTHER LEARNING

ON THE JOB QUALIFICATIONS ✦ PROFESSIONAL BODIES

NVQ/SNVQ level 1 BTEC HNC/HND Full-time/part-time/distance learning	e.g. HTF (Hospitality Training Foundation), INCI (Irish Hotel & Catering Institute)

CAREER OPPORTUNITIES

DEVELOPMENT OPTIONS

HIGHER EDUCATION ✦ MANAGEMENT ✦ FREELANCE

Well trained

The training you receive in catering will be dictated by what you actually want to do when you leave college or finish your apprenticeship. For example, a trainee baker will learn all about fermented goods (bread), while a trainee doing a course on food and drink service will learn all about carving, filleting and silver service skills. However, as so much of the catering industry is concentrated on what happens in the kitchen, let's take a look at some of the skills and disciplines you will learn there.

● **Health and safety**
Any kitchen where food is prepared for public consumption has to maintain strict hygiene levels – no one wants to be responsible for an outbreak of salmonella. Chefs and trainees must always keep the kitchen spotless and make sure there are no accidents that could contaminate the food being produced. Because of this the trainee's duties include an awful lot of washing and cleaning. Work surfaces must be washed down and kept sterile, and pots and pans must be thoroughly cleaned, as must crockery, cutlery and glassware. You will learn how to handle and maintain knives safely and at what temperatures certain fresh goods must be stored. You will also learn about hygienic storage of any prepared goods to be used at a future date.

● **Vegetable preparation**
One of the first things a trainee chef learns is different ways to prepare certain vegetables and fruits. You will find yourself slicing and dicing an awful lot of carrots, potatoes, cucumbers and more exotic items such as pineapples, mangoes and artichokes. Through practice, chefs learn to do this almost in their sleep and become exceptionally dextrous with their knives.

● **Fast food preparation**
Many courses recognise that a large number of trainees will go

into the fast food business, so training will include lessons on preparing food for frying, grilling, steaming and boiling.

● **Dressing plates**
Although at this stage you may not be actually cooking complicated dishes, the head chef may ask you to dress the plates before they leave the kitchen by adding garnishes, or by assembling some of the ingredients on the plate.

As you progress further (normally to NVQ Level 2) you will be learning new skills, such as:

● **Preparing and cooking meat**
You will have to learn all about boning, carving and recognising different cuts of meat, how to preserve them and how to cook them. You will also learn about the relevant sauces to go with each meat dish.

● **Preparing and cooking fish**
Most fish doesn't come into the restaurant ready prepared, so you will be taught to fillet, scale and clean a wide variety of different fish. You will also learn about different cooking techniques.

● **Dealing with deliveries**
At this stage you will need to know how to receive and handle food deliveries so they do not deteriorate in quality before being used.

Many courses will also teach you to cook basic pasta dishes, how to bake cakes and desserts, and also (in some cases) how to develop your knowledge of vegetarian food (a fast growing sector of the market).

By the time you get to train for NVQ Level 3 you will be involved in a much more sophisticated level of cooking, including shellfish, and marzipan, chocolate and pastry products, and you may also be taught about the use of wines and spirits.

9

Career opportunities

In the What's the Story? chapter, we looked at just some of the jobs open to people who enter the world of catering. You probably won't have a concrete plan of exactly where you want your career to go until you start training, but it is never too early to check out your options. For instance, you may begin by training in the kitchens only to discover you'd much rather be doing a job that brings you more into contact with the public. Alternatively, you may decide you are more interested in fine wines than food and decide to become a sommelier. Remember, the skills you learn as you train will stay with you for the rest of your life and will very much determine just how far you climb on the professional ladder. You may be quite content to reach the level of middle management, or your ambition could be to own and run a whole chain of themed bars. The Chief Executive of the Compass Group started in catering as a 16-year-old trainee chef, so just think how far you could go! The following diagram will give you a rough idea of what's actually out there for you and just how far you can go.

We have discussed most of these jobs already but there may be a few you don't recognise. A maître d'hôtel, or maître d', is a hotel or restaurant manager who greets customers or guests and ensures their visit or meal goes smoothly. The maître d' is very much the captain of the ship and is seen as the ambassador for his or her establishment.

Consultants tend to work for the big restaurant chains, but they can also be employed by smaller establishments. They give advice on all manner of details from how a restaurant should look (down to the shape of the plates and colour of the tablecloths), to what dishes will work. Many celebrity chefs, such as Gary Rhodes and Jamie Oliver, also act as consultants to big brand food producers and supermarket chains.

Private chefs are hired by individuals or big companies to cook exclusively for them. Many large country houses have their own private chefs, as do large companies where the chef cooks for the CEO or members of the board (especially if they do a lot of corporate entertaining). Other private chefs concentrate solely on cooking for private dinner parties.

In fact, a job in catering is a bit like food itself: it can be a simple meal of just one dish or a blow-out feast of five courses. What you make of it will very much depend on how far you want to go, but there are thousands of different opportunities out there for you, each offering both personal and financial rewards.

This is an industry with real opportunities for advancement. As you go through the training and discover where your strengths lie you will be able to map out a future career path. The diagram below shows options that will open up to you once you have trained.

CAREER OPPORTUNITIES

BASIC TRAINING IN CATERING

WAITER/WAITRESS ✦ COUNTER STAFF ✦ KITCHEN ASSISTANT

MORE TRAINING / NVQ LEVEL 1&2

TRAINEE CHEF ✦ SOMMELIER
RESTAURANT RECEPTIONIST ✦ HEAD WAITER

MORE TRAINING / NVQ LEVEL 3&4

MAITRE D' HOTEL ✦ MANAGER ✦ CONSULTANT
SOUS CHEF ✦ HEAD CHEF/HEAD COOK

10

The last word

If you have made it this far through the book then you will have probably made up your mind whether a career in catering is for you. If you think it is, then you have made a good choice. As Bill Vickers of the Compass Group says, 'a job in catering is fun, demanding, satisfying, rewarding and privileged – we have the opportunity to experience and be involved in things most of the general public may only dream of!' It is a career path that can take you a long, long way. But, before you start contacting the relevant bodies about your training options, on the next page is a fun guide to see if you really have got what it takes to succeed in the catering sector.

Catering is a career that really does have an amazing future. The fastest growing areas at present are contract foodservice and budget hotel businesses, and other major growth areas include themed public outlets, fashionable eateries, healthcare (National Health hospitals, private hospitals, clinics, and care homes), education, vending and casual dining. If you would like to work with people in a job that offers a wide variety and interesting experiences then this really is for you.

If you have made it this far through the book then you should know if **Catering** really is the career for you. But, before contacting the professional bodies listed in the next chapter, here's a final, fun checklist to show if you have chosen wisely.

THE LAST WORD ✔ TICK YES OR NO

DO YOU LIKE WORKING WITH YOUR HANDS?
☐ YES
☐ NO

DO YOU LIKE WORKING WITH PEOPLE?
☐ YES
☐ NO

DO YOU CONSIDER YOURSELF CREATIVE?
☐ YES
☐ NO

DO YOU WANT A JOB WHERE YOU WILL BE DOING SOMETHING DIFFERENT EVERYDAY?
☐ YES
☐ NO

ARE YOU SELF MOTIVATED AND ABLE TO THINK ON YOUR FEET?
☐ YES
☐ NO

ARE YOU ABLE TO COMMUNICATE EFFECTIVELY WITH LOTS OF DIFFERENT PEOPLE?
☐ YES
☐ NO

ARE YOU A SELF STARTER, ABLE TO TAKE CONTROL AND RESPONSIBILITY?
☐ YES
☐ NO

If you answered 'YES' to all these questions then
CONGRATULATIONS! YOU'VE CHOSEN THE RIGHT CAREER!
If you answered 'NO' to any of these questions then this may not be the career for you.
However, there are still some options open to you,
for example, you could work as a Waiter/Waitress, Bar Person or at a Food Counter

11

Resources

Listed below are all the addresses, telephone numbers and websites of the major government and industry bodies responsible for training in catering. There is also a list of publications you will find useful for background information and news on the industry.

TRAINING AND ADVICE
City and Guilds
1 Giltspur Street
London EC1A 9DD
020 7294 2468
www.city-and-guilds.co.uk

City and Guilds is the leading provider of vocational qualifications in the United Kingdom. It offers six types of qualification including NVQ and SVQ, Modern Apprenticeship (MA), Key Skills, Progression Awards, Higher Level Qualifications, Senior Awards, and its own City and Guild qualifications. The website gives comprehensive information on what courses are available and also where you can train.

Connexions
www.connexions.gov.uk
www.connexionscard.com

Connexions is aimed primarily at 13- to 19-year-olds, but is an excellent source of information for all ages. The Career Zone section includes a Career Bank that lists hundreds of careers with job descriptions and details on who to contact for more information.

Department for Education and Skills (DfES)
Packs available from 0800 585505
www.dfes.gov.uk

If you are undertaking a vocational training course lasting up to two years (with one year's practical work experience if it is part of the course) you may be eligible for a Career Development Loan. These are available for full-time, part-time and distance learning courses and applicants can be employed, self-employed, or unemployed. The DfES pays interest on the loan for the length of the course and up to one month afterwards. You can also find out which colleges are Centres of Vocational Excellence on the website www.dfes.gov.uk.coves.

Edexcel
Stuart House
32 Russell Square
London WC1B 5DN
0870 240 9800
www.edexcel.org.uk

Edexcel has taken over from BTEC in offering BTEC qualifications including BTEC First Diplomas, BTEC National Diplomas, and BTEC Higher Nationals (HNC and HND). It also offers NVQ qualifications. The website includes qualification 'quick links' and you can search by the qualification or the career you are interested in. Edexcel is currently being reorganised and all course and qualification information should be checked with them.

Food and Drink Qualifications Council
6 Catherine Street
London WC2B 5JT
020 7836 2460

Hospitality Training Foundation (HTF)/Hospitality Awarding Body (HAB)
International House
High Street
Ealing

London W5 5DB
020 8579 2400
www.htf.org.uk/www.hab.org.uk

Set up 30 years ago, the HTF represents hospitality employers
and gives information on education, training, skills, and
qualifications. On the website, look under Qualification Directory
for a comprehensive breakdown of the NVQs/SVQs and MAs
available in hospitality. HAB is the HTF's hospitality awarding
body branch and its website contains a comprehensive list of the
specialist hospitality qualifications it awards.

Hotel and Catering International Management Association (HCIMA)
Trinity Court
34 West Street
Sutton
Surrey SM1 1SH
020 8661 4900
www.hcima.org.uk

This is the hospitality industry's professional organisation for
managers and potential managers and is internationally
recognised. It offers its own professional Certificate and Diploma
for managers and more senior members of the industry.

Irish Hotel and Catering Institute
www.ihci.ie

This is the professional body for managers in catering in Ireland.

Learning and Skills Council
Modern Apprenticeship helpline
08000 150600
www.lsc.org.uk
www.realworkrealpay.co.uk

Launched in 2001, the Learning and Skills Council now has 48 branches across the country. It is responsible for the largest investment in post-16 education and training in England, including further education colleges, work-based training and workforce developments. Its realworkrealpay website is specifically aimed at those who would like to do Modern Apprenticeships.

For MAs in Scotland you should look at www.modernapprenticeships.com or www.careers.scotland.org.uk.

In Wales you should look at www.beskilled.net.

New Deal
www.newdeal.co.uk

If you are an older individual looking to change careers and you have been unemployed for six months or more (or receiving Jobseekers allowance), you may be able to gain access to NVQ/SVQ courses through the New Deal Programme. People with disabilities, ex-offenders, and lone parents are eligible before reaching six months of unemployment. Check out the website for more information.

Qualifications and Curriculum Authority (QCA)
83 Piccadilly
London W1J 8QA
020 7509 5555
www.qca.org.uk

In Scotland:

Scottish Qualifications Authority (SQA)
Hanover House
24 Douglas Street

Glasgow G2 7NQ
0141 248 7900
www.sqa.org.uk

These official awarding bodies will be able to tell you whether the
course you choose leads to a nationally approved qualification
such as NVQ or SVQ.

Springboard UK Ltd
3 Denmark Street
London WC2H 8LP
020 7497 8654
www.springboarduk.org.uk

Every industry should have its own equivalent of Springboard!
Springboard was set up to promote careers in hospitality, tourism
and leisure, and offers a specialist careers service giving free
advice. Each year it organises a week-long Careers Festival, and
a national cookery competition for 12- to 16-year olds entitled
'FutureChef'. It also offers work experience programmes, an
interactive CD-ROM called Springteractive, and an excellent
magazine entitled Career Compass, which you can also view at
www.careercompass.co.uk.

PUBLICATIONS
Caterer and Hotelkeeper
Quadrant House
The Quadrant
Sutton SM2 5AS
0208 652 3221
www.caterer.com

The main publication for the industry; it is packed full of features
and also advertises job vacancies. The website is an excellent
resource.

Catering South West
(part of the Newsquest South West group)
44 St James Street
Taunton TA1 1JR
01823 365151
www.cateringsouthwest.co.uk

Published ten times a year, this publication is exclusively for people working in hotels, pubs, restaurants, and fast food outlets in the South West.

Catering-uk.co.uk
Spring Grove House
Bewdley DY12 1LF
01299 403634
www.catering-uk.co.uk

This ezine is updated daily and covers all aspects of the catering industry.

Hotelier
(part of the Alliance Publishing group)
Adam House
Waterworks Road
Worcester WR1 3E2
01905 612733
www.hoteliermagazine.co.uk

Published six times a year: news and views on the hotel trade.

Scottish Caterer
Berguis House
20 Clifton Street
Glasgow G3 7LA
0141 567 6000
www.peeblesmedia.com

A monthly publication aimed at pub, hotel, restaurant and club staff across Scotland.